EASY
RECYCLING HANDBOOK

*What to recycle and
how to buy recycled...without
all the garbage.*

D1495365

Dee McVicker
Grassroots Books
Gilbert, Arizona

Published by
Grassroots Books
P.O. Box 86
Gilbert, Arizona 85299-0086

The information contained in this book is true and complete to the
best of the publisher's knowledge. No guarantees are made on the
results. The responsibilities lie with the reader.

Printed in the United States of America.

Book cover designed by Mark L. Woodruff.

Library of Congress Catalog Card Number: 93-79984
ISBN 0-9638428-5-4 $8.95 Softcover
First U.S. Edition 10 9 8 7 6 5 4 3 2 1

Publisher's Cataloging in Publication Data
McVicker, Dee
Easy Recycling Handbook/by Dee McVicker
Includes Index.
1. Recycling - citizen participation
2. Hazardous Waste
3. Compost

The text of this book is printed on recycled paper.

To Tonie Stanley

ACKNOWLEDGEMENTS

This book was made possible by many people. My deep gratitude goes to Professor David Pijawka of Arizona State University's Environmental Studies Center, who was a fountain of inspiration, ideas and information. I am grateful to Tommy Rowe with the Town of Gilbert, Arizona, whose encouragement guided the first pages of this book, and Donald Adams, who read the first draft with a thoughtful eye. Thanks to Pat Brown and the Stet Group: Dave Eskes, Nola Karel, Alan Korwin, Elizabeth Murfee, Ted Parod, Charles Sandford, Jr., and Mary Westheimer. Without their gentle prodding, this book would still be on the computer.

My thanks to Chris J. Warner of the Recycler's Hotline, Patricia Day and Richard Scott of Everything Earthly, Mary Norton of the Steel Recycling Institute, Wanda Wildman of the City of Phoenix, Mark O'Connor of the City of Mesa, Lisbeth Applefield of Source to Source Recycling, Eileen E. Miller, John D. Godec and Valerie M. Backus of the Arizona Department of Environmental Quality, John Ruston of the Environmental Defense Fund, Steven Katz, CRINC, National Office Paper Recycling Project, Elizabeth Adams, Christine Everhart Helfers and the many others who helped make this book possible.

A special thanks to my husband, Chuck, and our son, Dylan, for their understanding and support during the writing of this book; and thanks to my friends, Pauline Anderson and Reece Gilmore, who told me I could do it.

CONTENTS

Part One: GETTING STARTED

Part Two: WHAT TO RECYCLE

Part Three: WHAT TO DO WITH THE REST

Part Four: RECYCLING AT WORK

Part Five: BUYING RECYCLED

Part Six: 25 WAYS YOU CAN REDUCE WASTE

INTRODUCTION

Uncluttering used to be a favorite pastime of mine. The more I hauled away to the landfill, the better I felt. That was before I heard about Fresh Kills, a landfill on Staten Island where garbage is spread across 3,000 acres at 155 feet tall in some places. It is today one of the largest man-made structures in North America.

Someone once told me that Fresh Kills is visible from outer space. I'd never been to Fresh Kills, and certainly had never seen it from the porthole of a spaceship. But for days after I heard about it, I would try to imagine what 100 million tons of garbage actually looked like. Sometimes, as I imagined looking down on Fresh Kills from the earth's ether, I could actually smell garbage rotting.

From that time forward, I would never be able to see garbage in quite the same light again. I could no longer believe that everything I put into the trash disappeared, to be gobbled up like magic by a garbage truck. I knew that everything I throw away will exist at a Fresh Kills somewhere.

That's when I decided to recycle. I started out slowly at first. One aluminum can soon became 20, then 30. I purchased a tall trash container to store them in, still uncertain that I would ever fill it up. I did, many times. Little did I realize that I would eventually save from the jaws of trash not only pop cans, but newspapers, corrugated cardboard, plastics, papers of all kinds, and finally glass.

I wasn't alone. Others had spent thoughtful afternoons contemplating their Fresh Kills, too. People by the thousands were waking up and smelling the garbage.

Today, more and more of us are realizing that we can recycle without becoming fanatical environmentalists or sacrificing a lot of time to do it. The purpose of this book is to guide in that endeavor.

Part One

Getting Started

I was once told by a friend that recycling is a terrific idea, but not for her.

She was far too busy, she told me, with running the family business and mothering two active pre-schoolers. There were bills to pay, household chores to do, knees to bandage and all the other demands of active living that eclipsed the importance of recycling.

"I just simply don't have time," she complained.

It certainly seemed like a good argument, except it wasn't true. The fact is, my friend was recycling and had been for quite some time. Whenever she reused baby jars, donated to The Salvation Army or purchased post-consumed paper, she was recycling. As my friend soon learned, recycling isn't something we do. It's a process that each of us contribute to in varying degrees.

WHY YOU SHOULD RECYCLE

Reusing materials, or recycling, has been around as long as civilization. In fact, until modern times, recycling was more prevalent. This is probably because resources were scarce and people had to make do with what was available. Today, resources are more accessible and pliable than ever before. We have more widgets that do things for our convenience than ever in the history of man. Consequently, we also have more garbage, more pollution, and more strain put on our natural resources.

By now, you've heard that landfills are filling up rapidly, and soon there will be no place to dump our trash. But there are other problems. Leachate, a toxic mixture of water and decomposing garbage, is formed in landfills and has been known to find its way into community drinking water. Incinerating garbage doesn't appear to be much of solution, either. The leftover ash is also highly toxic.

Recycling is part of the solution to our landfill problems, and other ecological problems. When we recycle, we save on natural resources and contribute less to pollution. It takes less water and energy to reclaim recycled materials than it does to use virgin materials. In short, recycling helps to preserve forest woodland and maintain finite resources, ultimately contributing to the betterment of eco-systems that we are just beginning to understand.

WHAT IS ACTIVE RECYCLING?

With very little effort on your part, you can maximize the recycling process by becoming more active in it. This simply means separating materials from the waste stream, collecting them, and having them dropped off or picked up to be reclaimed and finally made into products you can purchase.

Sound like an inconvenience? It's not. Just ask the thousands of people who divert tons of waste annually from U.S. landfills to be recycled into cans, lawn chairs, newsprint, and more. Most of these people, like you and I, hold down jobs and lead active lives far from what could be termed sedentary.

BECOMING AN ACTIVE RECYCLER

As an active recycler, you now will be making informed purchasing decisions and contributing more to the recycling loop. How active you want to become is up to you. The idea is to fit as much of the recycling process into your lifestyle without overdoing it, a decision only you and your family can make. What might be ideal for your neighbor isn't always workable for your family. Some recycle aluminum only, others newspaper only, and still others recycle newspaper, aluminum, steel, and all the popular plastics. Most active recyclers change their recycling efforts as their lifestyles change.

To arrive at what's workable for your family, get acquainted with what your local government is doing about recycling and what community organizations are collecting. Assess how practical recycling will be given your family members, your living quarters and the materials you have to recycle.

If this sounds like more than you're willing to take on at the moment, start with the basics, such as aluminum cans or newspapers. You can always increase your efforts as you become more comfortable with recycling.

Of course, it's far better to reduce waste at the onset; that is, to buy less waste so you don't have to recycle it. No doubt, you're already doing this to some extent, if money has any influence over what you buy. This is called source reduction, a concept that goes hand-in-hand with recycling. Become aware of source reduction, and try to do more of it as you shop.

What's your local government doing?

Recycling is easiest by far if your local government has a recycling program — ideally curbside pickup. More than 2,500 communities around the nation now have curbside pickup of recyclables, in which residents can leave their recyclables at the curb each week to be collected by city trucks.

Many curbside recycling programs are mandatory, requiring residential communities to recycle. Others are pilot programs intended to test the waters of recycling before committing resources and money to a community-wide effort. Typically, only selected households in communities are asked to participate in pilot programs, although some allow households outside the pilot area to participate. You might have to pay extra for this convenience, often directly proportional to volume or weight of the materials you recycle.

 Some recycling programs provide special containers for your recyclables; others require that you bag materials to be taken with the trash each week. Some take a wide variety of materials commingled (such as plastics, papers, aluminum and tin); others take only one or two items, separated.

If your local government does not have a curbside program, perhaps it has other programs that will be of help. Is there a hazardous waste day at the local landfill for batteries and paint? Are dropsites available nearby for newspapers and cans? Perhaps your area's landfill has a compost so you can discard lawn clippings and other greens to be recycled into compost humus.

If you're not sure what is being done locally, contact your city's Public Works or Sanitation Department and ask for the recycling coordinator.

What's in your trash?

How will you know what to trash and what not to trash, particularly if there are no recycling programs in your community? Part of the answer is in your trash can.

Look through your trash. You'll be surprised at what you throw away: wrappers, beverage containers, glass jars. The majority of what households throw away is yard waste, followed by paper. We toss out plastic bottles in great numbers (Americans go through 2.5 million of these every hour!), as well as glass (we throw away enough glass bottles and jars to fill the twin towers of New York's World Trade Center every two weeks). Tons of aluminum, newspaper, iron, and steel also are thrown away on a daily basis.

Your trash can might fit this picture, or it might not. The important thing is to get a feel for what your family throws away. Even without being elbow deep in trash, you might have a pretty good idea. If you have a small baby, for example, it probably comes as no surprise that baby food jars are on the way to the landfill in abundance — along with disposable diapers.

Or, if your teenager is living up to his generation's reputation, you probably don't have to dig too deep before finding that pop cans or bottles are definitely not in short supply in your household trash.

Know thy "trash commodities"

Once you've arrived at a general idea of just what it is that makes its way from your house to the local landfill each week, start thinking about throw-aways in terms of nine major categories, or what I call *trash commodities,* as follows:

Newspapers
Aluminum (soda cans, TV dinner trays)
Tin (soup cans)
Glass
Paper (junk mail, grocery bags, cardboard)
Plastic (milk jugs, soda bottles, grocery bags)
Hazardous material

Compost (grass clippings, potato peelings)
Reusable clothing, furniture, household items

Studies show we can recover at least 50% of our waste by recycling. That's not to say you should commit yourself to such an ambitious undertaking. In fact, I highly recommend against it if this is your first venture into recycling. Instead, look for a trend, those items that are thrown away the most.

Questions to ask yourself: Are there more soda cans than soda bottles? Are your pop bottles glass or plastic? What about paper? Do you get a lot of junk mail? It will soon become apparent that your family's trash is made up of, say, more paper than soda cans, or more plastic milk jugs than cardboard containers.

WHERE TO DROP OFF MATERIALS

In your daily travels around town, keep your eyes open for bins, billboards, and other signs of recycling. The closer to your home or business, the better. In many cases the search for dropsites is a simple matter of becoming more aware of your surroundings. For example, perhaps there's a newspaper bin you pass by every day on the way to work but never noticed before.

Some states, like Arizona, have a hotline you can call with your zip code to find the nearest dropsite for various materials. In the future, consumers will be able to call a national hotline. Do take advantage of this clearinghouse. Not only will you save gas and time, but you'll likely garner helpful information on how local recyclers want their materials.

Recycling facilities vary according to what materials they take and how they take them. There are several general types: buy-back centers, retail stores, convenient dropsites, pickup services, and automotive.

BUY-BACK CENTERS: These takers of recyclables are in the business of brokering or reclaiming previously used materials, hopefully at a profit. Buy-back centers are listed under "Recycling Services" in the *Yellow Pages*, and will usually pay you a tipping fee for the materials you bring in. Some are non-profit organizations, often subsidized by cities, that encourage you to donate the money you make on recycling to a charity of your choice.

A buy-back center is likely to be your best choice if you're recycling a variety of items, or if you plan to get paid for your efforts. You might find, however, that buy-back centers are not as conveniently located as other dropsites.

RETAIL STORES: Some grocery stores and department stores take a few materials for recycling, such as milk and water jugs, aluminum cans, plastic and paper grocery bags, and cardboard. Ask your local grocer if the store is taking or plans to take in items for recycling. Even if you plan to visit a buy-back center once a month, you might want to take advantage of retailer bins for those items that stack up quicker than others.

CONVENIENT DROPSITES: If your grocer doesn't take items for recycling, there could be a corner of the grocer's parking lot that has a bin for newspapers, aluminum, or glass. If not, you're sure to find a bin or two near a busy intersection on your way home from the grocer. Some community parks also have them. These convenient dropsites are usually put out by charitable organizations, such as the Boy Scouts or the Lion's Club, or perhaps your city has invested in bins to encourage recycling in the community.

Convenient dropsites might not take all the items you're recycling, but they might be able to take the lion's share and free up space until you're ready to go to a buy-back center that is not as conveniently located.

PICKUP SERVICES: Recycling doesn't come much more convenient than hiring a pickup service to take your recyclables every week or two weeks. These services provide you with valuable tips on how to make recycling easier, and most are reasonably priced. If you're an apartment dweller, a pickup service is a great alternative that could ultimately lead to recycling throughout your entire complex. Ask your property manager about putting together a recycling program organized and handled by a professional recycler. Shop around for a service in the *Yellow Pages*, under "Recycling Services," or ask your local buy-back center to recommend one.

AUTOMOTIVE: Some auto supply and gas station

outlets accept used oil for recycling. Check with your mechanic the next time you have your car's oil changed. If you change your automobile's oil yourself, check with the clerk where you purchase your oil. While you're at it, find out if there are other automotive fluids you can recycle.

SETTING UP YOUR RECYCLING SYSTEM

If you're going to fit recycling into your lifestyle, you need a system that is easy enough to become routine for every member of your family. The ideal system will take into consideration the amount of space available, short-term and long-term storage, and the type of bins.

Make room

Space is the barometer by which you'll gauge how practical it will be to recycle the items you want to recycle. Not everyone has a garage or extended storage space for storing recyclable materials. But everyone, homeowner and apartment dweller alike, has a few feet of unoccupied space.

Look around your home. There are bound to be nooks and crannies that, with a little imagination, can stretch into the space you'll need for collecting recyclables. What about under the sink, inside a cupboard, above the washing machine or dryer?

Still hard pressed for space? Try replacing your

kitchen trash container with two smaller containers: one for garbage, the other for recyclables. After all, if you're going to be recycling 20 or 30 percent of your trash, you won't need the equivalent space for waste.

Establish collection points

As a matter of convenience, collect recyclables where they naturally accumulate. This might entail a two-step or three-step process to get materials collected and then stored until curbside pickup day or until you make a trip to the recycler.

Collect materials in a temporary container in the kitchen or living room, and then when these containers are full, empty the materials into a larger bin in the garage or wherever you can put a large 30- or 40-gallon container.

For example, paper from junk mail might be best collected in the foyer where you get the mail. It's easy to sort out the junk mail then and there to be collected in a recycling bin located next to your mailbox. (Better yet, rid your household of junk mail. Write: Mail Preference Service, Direct Marketing Association, P.O. Box 9008, Farmingdale, NY 11735-9008, to remove your name from direct mail lists.) Later, junk mail, along with other mixed papers you've collected at other locations in your home, can be stored in a larger container in the garage for delivery to a recycling center or dropsite.

Ideas for collecting materials:

- Bins attached to the inside of each cupboard door under the sink make for ideal collection points for materials used most often in the kitchen, such as tin cans, plastic jugs, glass jars.

- Catchall recycling bins next to garbage cans in the recreation room, or children's room, are great for temporary collection of all your recyclable items. Once a week sort through the materials.

- Store old newspapers close enough to the fireplace (where you probably read anyway) so you can use them for kindling, and for recycling.

- Put out matching, color-coded trash cans in bathrooms. A yellow trash can could hold the week's trash, and a green trash can could hold toilet roll tubes and other recyclables.

Long-term storage

The latest statistic is that each of us — man, woman, and child — throws away four pounds of trash every day. If a family of four recycles a quarter of its waste, the end result would be roughly 28 pounds to be taken to the recycler every week. For a family of two, the result is half as much at 14 pounds, still good cause to give some foresight to where you're going to store recyclables.

The idea is to store as much as you comfortably can in order to reduce the number of trips to your recycler. This will have a great deal to do with what you're recycling. Items that take up more bulk than others, especially those that add up fast such as milk and water jugs and plastic soda bottles, should be given first consideration in your search for space. The garage is where most look for this long-term storage. If you do not have a garage, don't give up hope. There's always the pantry, the carport, inside closets, or even outside if you have a waterproof container.

Next, look for nooks in closets or the garage that would hold those items that are less bulky or items not discarded in volume by your household. If you subscribe to only the weekend editions of the newspaper, for example, you might be able to store newspapers on a shelf in the pantry. Or, if your family purchases few canned goods, you might be able to place a small receptacle in the kitchen closet for tin cans.

If you're still faced with a space crunch problem, consider crushing cans, tamping down paper more often, or perhaps even sharing recycling bins with others in your apartment complex or community.

BINS YOU'LL NEED

Containers and bins come in all shapes and sizes, much like the items you'll be recycling. Some of the handiest are those made especially for recycling. These are typically stackable carton containers, which have front access or pull-out drawers and easy-grip handles.

Some are even available with wheels or attached dolly.

Look for these at your local hardware store or general merchandise store, and purchase the largest capacity your space will permit. Stack in the garage, or in the kitchen — where you're likely to collect most of your recyclables. Some stackable bins provide a means for labeling the bin according to recyclable material. If not, get them in various colors and color coordinate according to recycle commodity. A few even look good enough to blend in with your kitchen decor.

Garbage cans also work well, particularly the plastic lid-lock type. These usually come in various colors, 10 to 40 gallons, and are durable enough for items like glass and tin.

If you have tight spaces and the bulk of these bin containers just won't do, consider a drawstring bag system. They're lightweight, easy to store, and can be mounted on the wall or set up free-standing. These and other innovative containers are available through environmental catalogs (see Resources in the back of the book).

But, don't overlook containers you might already have around the house. I know of one recycler who uses large flour bins to store plastics, and another who uses an old milk crate to hold newspapers. What about an unused laundry basket, cardboard box or hamper? Or, an old rabbit cage for newspapers?

But before you settle on anything, keep one important rule in mind: make sure bins fit into your automobile or truck. If they don't fit, you'll be hard pressed to drop off materials at the recycler's.

GETTING THE FAMILY INVOLVED

In the best of all possible recycling efforts, family support is 100 percent. But don't hold out for this kind of commitment. Family members might feel inconvenienced at first, and can be downright resistant to recycling.

You'll need to assure them that recycling is simple. Then, get them involved at every opportunity. Ask for their input on what should be recycled, how it should be recycled and what they'd like to do to help. You might be surprised at how responsive they are, especially children, as my busy friend discovered. Not only were her children excited at the prospect of recycling aluminum cans, they were insistent, thanks to our nation's environmental awareness programs targeted to today's young people. If you're not getting this kind of response at home, perhaps a little bit of encouragement will help.

Make it fun

Make recycling a game for small children. Rounding up all the newspaper in the house, rinsing jars (and playmates!) with the backyard hose on a summer afternoon, or peeling labels from tin cans to be pasted together in a collage can be great fun for active children, and can burn off some of that youthful energy.

Make recycling tasks a special time for children. My busy friend's four-year-old looks forward to when his dad takes time out in the evening to crush the aluminum cans. His favorite part, he likes to tell anyone who will listen, is to operate the "crusher."

Get teens to chip in

For teens especially, recycling can be a great way to earn extra cash. By letting your teen cash in on, say, aluminum cans, you'll probably never have to worry about loading up the car for the recycling center — or getting together the cans to be recycled in the first place!

Make it educational

For children and adults of all ages, a trip to a landfill or materials recovery facility (MRF), where materials are recovered for recycling, is always an eye opener and loads of fun. You should encourage everyone in your family to come along. Ask your city's recycling coordinator or look in the *Yellow Pages* under "Recycling Services" for the address of the nearest MRF. Many of these places offer tours, so be sure to call ahead to find out when the tours begin.

Part Two

What To Recycle

NEWSPAPER

Americans recycle 18 million news-papers every day, the equivalent of about 200,000 trees.

No matter how you stack 'em, newspapers take up valuable real estate in landfills. That's one good reason to set them aside for recycling.

There are plenty of other reasons, not the least of which is newspapers are relatively easy to single out of the waste stream. This is why newspaper recycling is great for beginners, and why plenty of recyclers are recycling them. Currently, over a third of the newspaper in America is being recycled, and more newsprint mills are tooling up for recycling as more of us collect newspapers for this purpose.

Of course, newspaper recycling can take up valuable real estate in **your** home. To get a handle on newspaper recycling, try these helpful hints:

NEWSPAPER HINTS & STORAGE

BUNDLE WITH STRING. Two strings approximately four feet long (long enough to bundle a week's worth of newspapers) laid crisscross make for an easy way to transport newspapers. During the week stack used newspapers on the string, and tie at the end of the week.

IMPORTANT NOTE: Don't tie newspapers with wire, masking tape, or clothing. If this material makes it way into the paper printing process, it will be mixed in with pulp goo and will contaminate the batch.

BAG OR BOX. Brown paper grocery bags or cardboard boxes work great for containing newspapers. For bagging newspapers, simply turn the bag on its side, insert newspapers daily, and fill to a comfortable weight and bulk (usually a week's worth).

Another alternative: look through your recyclables for a suitable box. I managed to salvage two cardboard boxes that fit newspapers lengthwise and had handles on the end, so I could easily haul newspapers to the recycling center.

Some recycling centers prefer newspapers to be loose, others don't mind bagged or bundled newspapers, so do ask before you deliver your newspapers.

KEEP ON DRY LAND AWAY FROM DIRECT SUN. Few things are as heavy and unmanageable as soggy newspapers, so keep your stock as dry as your storage space will permit. Also, preserve your stockpile by keeping newspapers out of direct sunlight.

SEPARATE THE SLICK FROM THE PULP. There are two schools of thought on sorting out the glossy or stapled paper found in large supply in the Sunday newspaper. Many buy-back centers accept newspaper with all the slick trimmings, as long as junk mail and other papers have not been added. Many, however, would greatly appreciate a helping hand in sorting this material out. A good time to sort the slick from the pulp is as you're reading the paper.

NEWSPAPER TAKERS

You'll find quite a few takers for recyclable newspaper. Recycling drives by the Boy Scouts, the Lion's Club and other such organizations will gladly take them off your hands, as will bins set out by cities and recycling centers. Buy-back centers will, of course, pay you for your efforts.

Look in nearby shopping mall parking lots for newspaper bins, or at schools, parks and near busy residential areas. They're often white, easy to spot, and unmanned. If you're also recycling aluminum cans, you often can find a bin for aluminum cans at the same site as newspapers.

A way to remember it's time to make a trip to the bin: on your way to grocery shopping every week or two, or on the way to the gym on Saturday, load up your trunk with newspapers (and aluminum cans) and drop them off on the way.

ALUMINUM

More than 270 billion aluminum cans were recycled in the 1980s, accounting for approximately 50% of the aluminum beverage cans produced.

Not too many recyclers pass up aluminum cans. They're light, easy to store, and valued by buy-back centers, some of which will dole out good money for your aluminum. My mother-in-law regularly turns in her aluminum cans to a buy-back center and over the years has managed to pay for many landscaping extras, including part of a concrete block fence.

You probably will not get rich recycling beverage cans, even though aluminum is a finite resource. But you will be in good company. Aluminum is one of the most commonly recycled materials.

ALUMINUM HINTS & STORAGE

RINSE. Most centers and dropsites do not specify rinsed aluminum cans. But, with the bug population in many areas exceeding the human census, you might want to give cans the once-over before crushing.

Or, better yet, store cans in a container with a secure lid. This is also a good idea if you have small children, whose tiny fingers can get cut from the sharp edges of can openings. Occasionally you'll want to rinse out your container as well, to flush out sugary leftovers.

HAVE A CRUSH? If you live in cramped quarters, recycling cans can be made a lot more practical by getting a can crusher. Crushed cans take up about a quarter the space of uncrushed cans, which can proportionally cut the number of trips to the recycler if you live in a small apartment.

Can crushers are relatively inexpensive at $15 to $50, and some come with automatic feeders to make the task almost effortless. But before making the purchase, check with your recycling center. Some take cans that are crushed, others don't.

BI-METAL MEDLEY. A small percentage of beverage cans are made from a combination of aluminum, steel and tin. You'll be able to detect these by applying a refrigerator magnet to the can; if the magnet is attracted to it, the can is not made of aluminum and you'll need to check with your recycler on how to recycle it.

OTHER ALUMINUMS. Aluminum foil, screen doors, TV dinner trays, and aluminum bottle caps might be worth collecting with your aluminum cans, if your recycler gives you the go-ahead.

ALUMINUM TAKERS

If, like my mother-in-law, you're in it for the money, you can visit a buy-back center on a regular basis. Most of these recyclers will weigh your bulk on a scale and pay you what is referred to as a "tipping" fee, typically between 15 and 45 cents per pound, depending on current market value. Some buy-back centers advertise their rates, so check your local paper.

In some parts of the country, aluminum reverse vending machines will pay you based on the weight of aluminum you deposit. All cans should be emptied of their content.

If you're not cashing in, you'll have more takers for your aluminum. These might not pay you for your trouble, but they often make can collecting more convenient by placing dropsites in shopping malls and other convenient locations. Cities are especially aware of the convenience factor in recycling, and have drop-sites near schools and parks for this reason.

Still can't find a taker for your aluminum? Try Reynolds Aluminum Recycling hotline, number 800-228-2525, to find out where there's an aluminum handler near you.

TIN (STEEL) CANS

*Steel recycling saves Americans
more than $2 billion a year in waste
disposal costs.*

Most families have tin cans aplenty — as in containers for soups, vegetables, pet food. Actually, these cans are made more of steel than tin. Typically more than 99% of the can is made of steel. A thin layer of tin has been added to prevent rusting.

Both the tin and steel in these cans are recycled by steel mills, some by putting the can through a detinning process. The can is scrapped into pieces and the tin is removed chemically for use as fluoride in toothpaste, for example. The steel is then used to make other cans or used elsewhere, such as for automobile parts.

Tin/steel cans aren't as popular for recycling as aluminum, but they are starting to catch on as more of them are being collected by curbside programs and being reclaimed through magnetic separation at resource recovery facilities. Recycling these cans will earn you a place in this grassroots movement.

TIN/STEEL CAN SORTING HINTS

THE RIGHT STUFF. There are few hard and fast rules for recycling tin/steel cans, except one: make sure you're recycling the right stuff. Look for steel recycling symbols. One is three stars in a circle, another is a triangle also with three stars. Or, look for the word "steel" on the product, such as "Steel. Please Recycle." That failing, try a magnet. Steel is magnetic, aluminum is not. Another way to tell the difference: tin/steel cans typically have rivets or ribs on the side and aluminum cans do not.

CHECK LIDS. Some tin/steel cans have aluminum lids, which some recycling centers will take along with your tin/steel cans and others will not. Many curbside recycling programs and recycling centers take tin/steel cans with the lids tucked inside. Ask your recycler.

AEROSOL AND PAINT CANS. Your refrigerator magnet will give you the go-ahead to include aerosol cans, but your regular recycler might not. These cans have a reputation for being difficult to recycle, in part because there has not been a widely accepted set of instructions for recycling them. Even so, today there are well over 500 recycling programs that include empty aerosol cans, and a number of curbside programs that include empty paint cans.

TIN/STEEL CAN STORAGE HINTS

RINSE, PEEL OR SQUASH? Most recyclers will take cans unflattened and with the label on, although you'll want to check with your recycling center to find out for sure. You should rinse cans, though. I find it easiest to rinse cans immediately after use. If you have a particularly filthy can, you can always prop it in the dishwasher for a washing instead of wasting valuable time and water at the sink. If you don't have a dishwasher, rinse cans in dish water after you've washed the dinner dishes.

FORGET THE RUST. If you hang on to tin/steel cans long enough, or leave them near the water sprinkler, they'll probably rust. Don't worry about this. They're still good for recycling and recyclers will take them just the same.

TIN/STEEL CAN TAKERS

Buy-back facilities are the most likely candidates for your tin/steel cans, many of which will give you a modest payment for your efforts.

If there is not a buy-back facility near you, try scrap metal facilities. Look in the *Yellow Pages* under "Scrap Metal."

Or, call the Steel Can Recycling Hotline sponsored by the Steel Recycling Institute, number 800-937-1226, for a nearby dropsite.

GLASS

Approximately 1,250,000 tons of glass, or 5 billion containers, are recycled annually in the United States.

The best plan I know of for glass is the one my grandmother used. Before throw-away bottles were the norm, Grandma used to return her glass bottles to the grocer for refills. And, every week she set her milk bottles out for the milkman for the same purpose.

Today, trying to find affordable, refillable bottled beverages is like trying to find a horse-drawn cab in New York City. But, affordable refillables could be coming back around. Since Oregon passed the first bottle bill in 1972, at least 10 states have followed with similar laws that mandate a five- to 10-cent deposit on certain beverage bottles to be redeemed when returned. Bottle bills, in essence, encourage the continual reuse of glass beverage bottles.

Ideally, all glass containers should be refilled and reused in this way. But, since this isn't practical for every glass jar, bottle or container that finds its way into your household, you'll need to do some glass recycling.

GLASS HINTS & STORAGE

ALL GLASS IS NOT CREATED EQUAL. Do not include window glass, glassware, light bulbs, or ceramic wares in your glass recycling. These need to be handled separately if a recycler takes them, or they need to be given to a salvage yard. The recipe for these glasses is very different from that of the glass in bottles and jars used for foods. Ceramic, for example, is made from fine rock particles, whereas light bulb glass is made with more soda ash.   Moreover, glass used to contain food in bottles and jars is melted at 2,600° Fahrenheit, a temperature that will not melt ceramic.

If you're not sure if the material is recyclable, it's better to not include it in your glass recyclables. Getting these mixed in with recyclable glass can ruin large vats of glass on the way to glass manufacturers.

EMPTY AND RINSE. Rinsing with water is good; running it through the dishwasher along with your dishes is even better. If you run glass jars through the dishwasher, a word of warning: peel off the label. Flakes of paper stuck to your entire dishwasher load is a mess you'll likely not forget.

REMOVE CAPS, NECK RINGS. Take these off if at all possible. Caps made of plastic or metal are of little use to glass makers, and glass makers have even less use for bottleneck rings made of wire or plastic. Some caps and lids can be recycled along with your tin cans or aluminum cans.

LABEL, LABEL. You can leave the labels on glass jars. Most recyclers will accept them this way, as many can vacuum off labels easily enough. But it is just as easy for you to do it.

COLOR COORDINATE. You may have already noticed that glass bottles and jars are clear or come in shades of brown or green. These are the colors that marketers tell us we like. Consequently, in order to increase the marketability of recycled glass, some recyclers like us to color sort our bottles and jars according to brown, blue or clear.

IMPORTANT NOTE: Even slightly tinted glass should not be recycled with clear glass. Recycle these with the appropriate color.

Other recyclers and many city curbside programs are a bit more forgiving and let you mix glass colors. In some cases, they sort by color for you in order to market your glass to glass makers, or they simply market your mixed colored glass to glass makers who aren't particular about color. Manufacturers of fiberglass insulation, for example, use mixed glass as could a bottler who makes an "ecology bottle" of mixed colors — a great idea that hopefully will catch on.

DON'T BREAK. One slip-up isn't shattering, but most recyclers like bottles and jars intact. The more breakage, the harder it is for recyclers to handle. This translates into higher costs at the grocery counter when consumers go to pay for goods made from recycled glass.

You can keep breakage to a minimum by using inflexible containers rather than bags to store glass. Containers with handles also make it easier to move glass, since even a tiny load can be bulky and heavy.

NO SIX-PACKS. Scratch the idea of keeping beverage bottles in their six-pack carriers. This is just added handling work for recyclers.

PAPER

Over 30%, or more than 26 million tons, of all the paper and paperboard used in the United States is being collected and utilized.

There's plenty of opportunity to recycle paper, and plenty of ways to do it. So where do you start? In theory, a good start is with the brown papers, such as paper bags and cardboard boxes. After you've mastered these, move on to telephone books and/or magazines, and finally mixed paper. But in practice, some find it easier to start with mixed paper recycling, although it's not the most efficient way to recycle paper. Whichever your approach, your efforts will be well rewarded. Every ton of paper that's recycled saves three cubic yards of material in the landfill. Moreover, recycling a ton of paper uses 40% less energy than making the equivalent from virgin paper — saving enough electricity to power the average American home for five months!

Mixed paper

The good news is that very few paper items are eliminated from mixed paper recycling, but the bad news is that the grade of paper produced from this mix is not all that great. The idea, then, is to maintain a standard to keep this large volume of paper marketable to recyclers.

Here are a few do's and don'ts of mixed paper recycling:

DO INCLUDE:
Junk mail
Glossy, slick paper
Paperboard such as cereal boxes, toilet roll tubes
Wrapping paper
Stationery
Paper grocery bags (if you're not recycling separately)

DON'T INCLUDE:
Toilet tissues
Paper plates
Facsimile Paper
NCR paper (carbonless)

Bubble envelopes
Foil wrapping paper

MIXED PAPER TIPS

The rules for mixed paper recycling are few, but definitely worth following if you're taking on this bulk.

GET RID OF THE EXCESS. Remove staples and glue backing. The best time to do this with junk mail is when you're sorting through the mail.

Don't forget to get rid of the plastics from envelopes, the wax or plastic linings in cereal boxes, and food waste (try rinsing). Also, get rid of metal clasps on envelopes and paper clips on papers, and pull off as much tape as you can.

COLLECTING MIXED PAPER. A short-term mixed paper receptacle is definitely suggested for your kitchen or laundry room, unless you can store a large bin close by. Not only will it save you extra trips to the bin in the garage or carport, but it will save temptations by family members to throw away good recyclables.

STORING MIXED PAPER. Mixed paper adds up, especially if it's the only paper recycling you're doing. To store this bulk, get the largest container your storage space will allow but not too big that it's too heavy to lift when full, and tamp down often.

Brown paper & boxes

You can recycle all brown, or kraft, paper together. This includes:

Paper Bags: These are the grocery store kind, the very same that you stash under the kitchen sink to be used for who-knows-what.

Brown Cardboard: These are packing boxes, such as the box the new stereo came in, and the boxes used for moving. In recycler-ese these are called corrugated cardboard, and this material is in high demand and in short supply, so do recycle.

BROWN PAPER/BOXES TIPS

FLATTEN BOXES. This is easy. Just cut bottom tape seams with a jackknife and let the box naturally fold flat. Keep a jackknife hanging on a string near your box stash for this purpose.

REMOVE STAPLES AND GLUE, and pull the remainder of the tape off. Wood, plastic and string will have to go, too.

NO PLASTIC BOXES, PLEASE. Corrugated boxes with a plastic coating just do not mix well with straight corrugated boxes in the recycling process.

FORGET THE GREASE. If you order your pizzas extra greasy, it's best to forget trying to recycle these pizza boxes.

STORING BOXES. It will probably take you a while to build up enough boxes to justify a trip to the recycler, unless you've made a move recently. I have found the best way to store cardboard boxes is either in an oversized box salvaged for this purpose, or inside the garage or carport against the walls.

You can bundle boxes together with twine, which might even be required if you're participating in a curbside pickup program. If not, your recycler might want you to remove the twine once you arrive at the dropsite.

STORING PAPER BAGS. Paper bags can store along with your cardboard boxes in an oversized box you've set aside, or under your sink as they always have. Use one paper bag, or a small cardboard box, to hold the other bags.

COLORED BAGS AND WHITE BAGS do not mix with browns, so recycle these separately or as mixed paper.

PAPER TAKERS

Cardboard & Grocery Bags: Some grocers pay a nickel or more for grocery bags, and those that have balers to reclaim cardboard might take your boxes.

Check with your local grocer.

Phone Books. If you live in a metropolitan area, each set of phone books you receive is likely to contain at least two volumes with over a thousand pages each — a weighty reason for recycling them.

Telephone companies have also done the math, and in the last several years have begun to provide a means for recycling phone books. Now, with your new phone books, you'll probably find a note that instructs you where to drop off last year's phone books for recycling. If not, you might want to call your telephone company's customer service department for details on where you can drop off old telephone books. That failing, you can recycle your telephone books as mixed paper.

Magazines. Some recycling centers take magazines as a single recyclable product, others mix magazines in with mixed papers. If you find a recycler who recycles magazines separately, he or she will appreciate you doing the following:

Don't recycle other glossy paper with magazines. It might all look the same, but the paper for each can be quite different.

No newsprint, please. This is the newspaper-type paper found in some TV guides and some trade publications.

PLASTIC

In 1990, 225 million pounds of PET plastic were recycled, representing 30% of all PET soft drink bottles produced.

Plastic recycling, we've been told, is tricky business. There's PET and HDPE, soda bottles and detergent jugs. Some types can be recycled together, others can't. And to top it off, few of us can tell the difference between one type of plastic and another.

No wonder it's so tempting to forego plastics recycling, which plenty do — for awhile. But most of us get around to recycling plastics eventually. The number of plastics products used in the home today is certainly good enough reason to give it a try.

Then what? First, relax. After all, you're not making plastic; you're recycling it. Next, get acquainted with the standard coding system developed by the Society of the Plastics Industry, which suggests that plastics be identified by resin type. Since this system of categorizing plastics by type came along several years ago, plastics recycling has become almost as easy as counting to seven.

According to the Society of the Plastics Industry, plastics can be grouped into seven types of resins, each best suited for different uses. PET resin, for example, can hold in carbonation and therefore is used for making soda bottles. HDPE, on the other hand, is better for containers with handles and therefore is used for making milk jugs.

Best of all, when it comes time to recycle, all you have to do is check the number on the container to know the type of plastic and how to recycle the product. Usually, the standard recycling logo with a number stamped in the middle along with the type of resin is seen on or near the bottom of the container.

Plastic soda bottles, for example, are identified by the number 1 and PETE for this resin type. The following is a list of the types of plastics. After you've become comfortable with recycling one group of plastics, try refining your system to include more and more types.

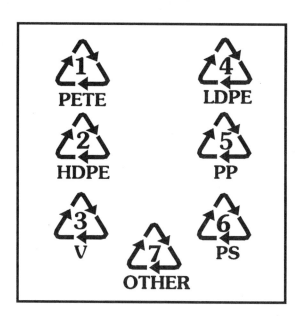

1 (PET or PETE)

This is a popular plastic that is now in high demand by recyclers. Chances are you have quite a few products in your home that are made of this resin, referred to as *polyethylene terephthalate* (PET).

PRODUCTS OR CONTAINERS
MADE OF PET, 1

2-LITER POP BOTTLES: All soda bottles are made of PET plastic simply because this particular plastic is ideal for carbonated beverages.

PLASTIC LIQUOR BOTTLES: All liquor containers are also made of PET.

SOME VEGETABLE OIL CONTAINERS. Be careful:

these containers could instead be made out of *polyvinyl chloride*, or PVC, a small amount of which can be catastrophic to a vat of PET. One way to tell if it's PET: PET bottles never have seams and often have a raised dot at the center of the base.

SUGGESTION: Rinse containers lightly, and remove the caps to be recycled separately.

2 (HDPE)

This is the symbol for *high-density polyethylene* (HDPE), a lightweight and rugged plastic.

PRODUCTS OR CONTAINERS
MADE OF HDPE, 2

MILK JUGS

BUTTER CONTAINERS

DETERGENT AND BLEACH BOTTLES

SOME DAIRY CONTAINERS SUCH AS COTTAGE CHEESE TUBS, but only if you see a number 2 at the bottom since these containers can instead be made out of *polystyrene* (PS, number 6).

SOME PLASTIC GROCERY BAGS, but only if they make a crinkle noise when you wad them up. Some plastic bags are made of LDPE plastic, number 4.

SUGGESTIONS: Remove milk and water jug caps and collars. These are made of polypropylene plastic, 5, which is not widely recycled. Rinse containers, remove all labels and flatten. Some recyclers prefer you to sort HDPE by clear or color, so do ask.

3 (V)

This container is usually shiny, tough and when bent, shows a white crease. The technical term for this plastic is *polyvinyl chloride*, or PVC, a vinyl.

PRODUCTS OR CONTAINERS
MADE OF V, 3

SHAMPOO BOTTLES

WATER BOTTLES, but not the water jugs, the imported water kind.

CREDIT CARDS

LUNCH MEAT FILM. Not too many food products are packaged in PVC film, but luncheon meat and cheese are the exception.

SUGGESTIONS: Remove caps and collars of bottles (which are typically made of polypropylene, number 5, and not widely recycled). Rinse, remove all labels and flatten.

IMPORTANT NOTE: Keep PVC separate from other plastics. PVC mixed with PET in the plastics-making process can wreak havoc on machinery.

4 (LDPE)

Chances are you're coming in contact with a good

many products made out of *low-density polyethylene*, or LDPE, during the course of your day. LDPE, which the Society of the Plastics Industry symbolizes as code 4, is most often seen in its filmy form, such as plastic wrappings on foods and dry cleaning.

PRODUCTS OR CONTAINERS
MADE OF LDPE, 4

PLASTIC GROCERY BAGS, but only the ones that *do not* make a crinkle noise when you wad them up. LDPE bags are usually more elastic.

PLASTIC SANDWICH BAGS

MOST SHRINK-WRAP PACKAGING for compact discs, games, food products.

SUGGESTIONS: Not all LDPE bags are stamped with the code, in fact very few are, so you'll have to check with your recycler on these. **DO NOT INCLUDE cling wrap or cellophane in with LDPE plastics, which have added ingredients unsuitable for LDPE recycling.**

5 (PP)

This is usually an opaque plastic, commonly used as lids and caps on jars and bottles. It's called *polypropylene*, and unfortunately, not too many local recyclers take it.

PRODUCTS OR CONTAINERS
MADE OF PP, 5

SYRUP BOTTLES

COTTAGE CHEESE AND YOGURT CONTAINERS

MAJORITY OF PLASTIC BOTTLE CAPS AND LIDS

DRINKING STRAWS

SUGGESTIONS: Your local recycler might not take this plastic, but do check the Yellow Pages for a multi-material buy-back facility in your area that will. Save caps and lids for a semi-annual trip to a buy-back facility.

6 (PS)

When archaeologists dig through our landfills centuries from now, they no doubt will notice our passion for fast food. That's because *polystyrene* (PS), which is better known as Styrofoam™ and is commonly used to package fast foods, will still be with us. This plastic simply does not biodegrade.

The challenge, then, is to either do away with PS entirely or to recycle it. If you decide to recycle, there are several programs now in place or in the developmental stages that can help. Schools, fast-food restaurants, and other institutions are now collecting this material to be cleaned and converted into pellets for building insulation, for example.

There also are hundreds of outlets now taking foam

packing material to be recycled. Check with your local mail service bureau, or call the Association of Foam Packaging Recyclers at 800-944-8448.

PRODUCTS OR CONTAINERS
MADE OF PS, 6

STYROFOAM™ CUPS AND PLATES

FOAM FAST-FOOD CONTAINERS

FOAM COFFEE CUPS

FOAM PACKING MATERIAL, SUCH AS PACKING PEANUTS

MOLDED FOAM FOR PACKAGING GOODS SUCH AS ELECTRONICS COMPONENTS

7 (OTHER)

Not all products or containers are made of one type of plastic. Some are commingled with other types of plastics, which is why the Society of the Plastics Industry saw fit to include "other" in their coding system. The number 7 product could also be made of a rarely used plastic type, and should be purchased sparingly by consumers since it is not readily recyclable.

Part Three

What To Do With The Rest

COMPOSTING

Increasingly, communities are organizing programs to compost yard waste.

A solid quarter of family waste is material that could be made into usable compost soil. Composting is how nature naturally recycles organic materials. When leaves fall to the ground, nature immediately begins the process of converting this organic lifeform into a rich soil that, in turn, is used to grow new life.

You might want to help nature along by building a compost pile and occasionally stirring it or watering it if you're living in an arid climate.

Composting is something family members can do together, much like tending to a garden. In fact, if you have a garden, compost humus is a great soil additive for growing healthy vegetables and flowers.

If your family doesn't have a garden, you can always give your humus to landscapers, local farmers or a nearby food co-op, all of which are in the market for new sources of rich organic compost to grow their crops.

What can you compost?

Just about anything organic, except domestic animal droppings. Dog, cat, or other domestic animal excrements could carry diseases that could contaminate your compost, a problem especially if you want to use your compost humus in your vegetable garden. Also, scratch diseased green clippings as these likewise can spread disease.

You might want to ban meat, fat, and bones from your compost pile, since these can be an invitation to wild animals. These materials also give off a foul odor once they start fermenting in the soil, and take longer to break down than other, more suitable organics.

Suitable material to put in your compost pile are garden waste and some table food scraps. The greater variety of organic materials, the better.

Here are just a few examples of what you can compost:

> Grass clippings
> Hay or straw
> Tree or plant leaves
> Garden plant greens or weeds

Vegetable scraps
Fruit scraps
Dog/cat food
Coffee grounds
Tea
Crushed rock (dust)
Pasta and bread remains
Paper towels (and paper towel holders!)

Why compost?

There are many reasons to compost; here are three:

- Composting enables you to recycle organic waste that would otherwise sit in the landfill, unable to decompose as nature intended.

- Composting saves the hassle and cost of buying potting soil, fertilizer and mulch.

- Compost is good for your plants. It holds moisture in and promotes good soil drainage. Plus it adds nutrients to the soil which are healthy for your plants.

Three easy steps to composting

Composting is a fun, exciting and complex science. There are many ways to compost, and just as many good books on the subject. The following is one approach to composting. You might want to expand on your knowledge of composting by visiting your local bookstore or library.

1. Find a shaded area in your yard to set up your compost bin. Under a tree is good, but not too close to the house or garage. Active composting will rot the wood.

2. Set up a compost bin. Plenty of composters don't use a compost bin, but one is recommended as it tends to keep the pile moist and free from pests. Your bin can be made of wood, chicken wire, or metal, depending on what you have available. A cover, such as a tarp, is always a good idea to keep too much rain from leaching microorganisms out of the compost pile.

Here are a few suggestions for compost bins:

Cinder block, or stacked brick, bin

A cylinder of fencing or chicken wire *(wire openings of less than two inches work best)*

Wood pallets nailed together to make a pen *(use three or four pallets)*

Large trash can *(cut bottom off and puncture with holes)*

Perforated steel drum

A hole dug into the earth

Compost bin *(look through environmental catalogs)*

Wood siding nailed together to make a large box

Community bin shared by others in your neighborhood or community. Call your local landfill to find out if there is one.

IMPORTANT NOTE: If you decide to use wood for a compost bin, check to make sure the wood is preserved with a compound non-toxic to plants. Wood preservatives that are toxic to plants are unsuitable for composting. If you treat the wood yourself, copper naphthenate is an excellent choice.

As for the size of your compost, a good rule of thumb is that for every square foot of vegetable or flower bed garden you have, you'll need one pound of compost humus. If you have a 500 square foot garden, for example, you'll easily use around 500 pounds of humus. A 3 x 3 foot compost bin will give you this amount every few months to a year, depending on your location and how serious you are about composting.

3. Layer in equal parts greens and browns. Browns are items such as dead leaves, wood shavings, straw. Greens are fresh grass clippings, pulled weeds, and food scraps. Spray on a little bit of water. The pile should be moist, but not wringing wet.

Crumple leaves and tear food scraps and other items you put in the compost into little pieces so the pile can "digest" it easier.

Helpful Hint: Since your compost will need nitrogen to get it really cooking (compost heaps can reach 130° to 160° Fahrenheit!), you can add one-half to a full shovelful of steer or horse manure as a jump-start. Get this at your local plant nursery. Or, add a bit of store-bought compost to the pile. There are also compost starter kits that can do much the same thing. These are available at your local plant nursery or hardware store.

What will I have to do once I start my compost pile?

Keep adding yard waste, water if needed, and stir on occasion (once or twice a week should do it). Pitchforks, rakes, long poles, and shovels are good stirring tools. Always shred waste before putting into the bin, and moisten with a light spray of water.

If you don't want to stir too often, consider putting old tree branches at the bottom of your compost to aid in aerobic decomposition. Worms also can be added to cut down on how often you need to stir. Your brewing compost will probably be an open invitation to a few worms in the neighborhood, who will no doubt find living conditions suitable enough to raise their families and supply you with generations of worms (eight worms can multiply to 1,500 in six months!). If not, you can purchase worms at a bait shop. Red worms, sometimes called "red wrigglers" or "manure worms," thrive best in the compost. Be sure to put worms on the edge of your pile, as the temperatures are too high to support worm life at the core.

WORM COMPOSTING: If you live in an apartment or don't want to commit to a backyard compost, consider worm composting. Here's how: put a few worms in a sturdy wooden box with lid, fill the box with a bedding of newspaper, corrugated cardboard, peat moss or leaves, and add food wastes such as fruit peels, breads, and grain. Soon you'll have worm compost to put in your potted plants.

USES FOR COMPOST:

POTTING SOIL MIX: Sift compost through a 1/2" screen and mix two parts of the sifted compost with one part sand. Or, add to commercial soil at a ratio of one part compost to two parts commercial soil.

SOIL ENRICHER: Mix compost into vegetable and flower gardens along with fertilizer at the start of every growing season. Mix in with the topsoil when planting new trees and shrubs. Compost will promote good drainage and keep moisture in, as well as provide some of the nutrients your plants need.

MULCH: A layer of mulch spread 1/2 inch deep over gardens and on tree and shrub basins will keep plants moist in dry climates and keep soil from eroding in wet climates.

GIVING TO CHARITIES

Americans send about 135,000 tons of used clothing to Third World countries every year.

In late 1800s England, it was common to find a man and his horse-drawn carriage roving the back streets in search of discarded household items. They called him the rag-and-bone man, and city dwellers could always count on him to take their used furniture and other household items to be refurbished and sold to those in need.

Today, in modern America, we too have a rag-and-bone man in the form of Goodwill Industries, The Salvation Army, St. Vincent de Paul Society, and other thrift shops and organizations. Many of these organizations have trucks parked at local shopping centers on certain days for you to drop off cloths or smaller items. Most will arrange to pick up whatever large items you might have. When giving to these organizations, always ask for a receipt that can be used come income tax time to show that you've donated to a charity.

What to give to charities

CLOTHES: If you decide to join the thousands in this country offering their used clothes for charity, take the time to wash cloths first. It doesn't take much effort and can save precious time and resources for the volunteers who pass your clothing on to those in need.

APPLIANCES: Stoves, microwave ovens, refrigerators, toasters, air conditioners, and the like are often in demand by non-profit charitable organizations. Many will even take repair items, which they fix and sell. All you have to do is make the call.

HOUSEHOLD GOODS: Furniture and household goods such as curtains, bedding and rugs are the mainstay of just about every thrift organization.

Where to call

Look in the *Yellow Pages* under "Thrift Shops."

HAZARDOUS MATERIALS, AUTOMOTIVE & OTHER MISCELLANY

Of the total oil generated each year for automobiles, approximately one-third is recycled.

Every family has hazardous materials, whether it be household cleaning products, car batteries, automotive fluids like oil and antifreeze, paint, solvents, pesticides, or weed killers.

It is estimated that American families produce four million pounds of household hazardous waste everyday. We buy 140 million gallons of latex paint, dump out 21 million pounds of antifreeze, and stockpile 280 million scrap tires — one for each person — each year. There are well over two billion discarded tires piled up around the country, and even though we are recycling more motor oil than ever, Americans still throw away enough motor oil every year to fill 120 supertankers. The list of hazardous horrors goes on every day. By far, the best alternative to hazardous materials is not to buy them to begin with, or at least, to purchase and use them sparingly. Your efforts in this area will not only help the environment breathe easier, it will save disposal costs.

The Seattle Solid Waste Utility publishes that for every gallon of paint or paint thinner, it costs $3.55 to safely dispose of it. Toilet bowl or oven cleaner costs $4.00 per gallon for safe disposal, and weed-killer costs over $11.00 per gallon for safe disposal.

The city suggests Seattle residents buy only the amount needed, use up as much of the product as possible (or give the leftovers to someone who will), and try to choose safe products over products containing toxic or hazardous materials.

That failing, dispose of properly.

COMMON HOUSEHOLD WASTE

When disposing, it's common practice to keep hazardous waste in its original container. Some products have label instructions for disposal that you can follow. Many cities and communities have designated days when you can drop off or leave certain hazardous materials at the curb for pickup. Call your city's Sanitation Department for the days and the materials taken.

*IMPORTANT NOTE: DO NOT pour your haz-
ardous waste down the drain, where it can
go untreated into nearby lakes and streams.*

PAINT: Paint is considered a hazardous material, and it's no longer a safe alternative to just
throw away your leftover paint. Take this five-step
approach to recycling or disposing of household
paint properly:

*1) Divide the moldy and dried-out paint from
the still usable paint. If the paint is unusable,
dispose of it at your local hazardous waste
facility.*

*2) Divide paint according to whether it's oil-
based or latex, and interior or exterior paint.*

*3) Try mixing latex paints together. The result
might be a beige or gray color, which could
make a good primer.*

*4) Swap or recycle. Find a place that recycles
paint by contacting your local Sanitation Department or waste management facility. Some let
you exchange paint for paint of a different color.*

*5) The next time you buy paint, steer clear of
oil-based types, which contain hydrocarbons.
Latex or water-based paints are better, especially those that do not have added fungicides
(some of these fungicide paints contain mercury). Better yet, ask for paints containing bees-*

wax, carnauba wax, and plant extracts, which are environmentally friendly.

SUGGESTION: Don't throw away paint thinner with each use. Save in a jar for reuse; the sediment will sink to the bottom. When disposal does become necessary, dispose of as you would any hazardous material.

HOUSEHOLD BATTERIES: Regular household batteries DO NOT belong in your trash can. They contain toxic materials, including mercury. Check around at various recycling centers, or outlets where you purchase batteries, to find out if there is a program to recycle household batteries in your area. Battery recycling has caught on in Japan and parts of Europe, and is just now catching on in the United States, possibly in your community. If not, dispose of as you would any hazardous material by contacting the waste disposal branch of your local government.

The next time you're in the market for batteries, purchase re-chargeable batteries, or look for the new mercury-free batteries now on the shelf.

ASBESTOS & ASBESTOS-CONTAINING MATERIAL: Removal of house siding or pipe insulation that contains asbestos will release asbestos fibers, which are a known cause of lung cancer and other respiratory problems. Contact your city government for safe removal.

BUILDING MATERIAL: Incredible as it may sound,

plain old building material can be toxic in landfills. Some plywood and particle boards contain *formaldehyde*, an environmental hazard that when exposed to high temperatures will release a toxic fume. Other building materials are treated with chemicals for preservation and insect deterrence, so do check with your local Sanitation Department before disposing of building material.

PESTICIDES & HERBICIDES: If you must use toxic pesticides or herbicides, use sparingly and NEVER dump down the drain or sewer but discard according to instructions by your local Sanitation Department.

The next time, consider using traps or environmentally safe pesticides. Better yet, make your yard inviting for ladybugs, lizards, frogs or birds. They'll get rid of the pests for you (some plant nurseries and hardware stores sell ladybugs and other such critters for this purpose). Instead of using herbicides, pull weeds by hand. And don't cut grass too short in order to choke out weeds.

COMMON AUTOMOTIVE WASTE

MOTOR OIL & OTHER FLUIDS: Do not dump onto the ground, into the garbage, or down drains. If you change your car's oil yourself, check with your local Sanitation Department to find out if there's curbside pickup of motor oil. Or, bring all used motor oil to the nearest gas station for recycling. Some automotive retailers and quick oil-change marts also take motor oil. If you have your oil changed by a gas station or automotive retailer, be sure to find out first if they plan to recycle your oil.

Some of these outlets also take other automotive fluids such as antifreeze and transmission and brake fluid. Do not mix automotive fluids, but keep motor oil, antifreeze, and other fluids separate.

SUGGESTION: The next time you get your car's air conditioner serviced, ask your mechanic if he recycles chlorofluorocarbon (CFC) coolant. New devices, endearingly called vampires, suck out CFC coolant when servicing home and automobile air conditioners and collect this ozone-depleting chemical for recycling.

TIRES: Did you know that if you throw your old tires out, it will take at least 800 years for them to decompose? Whole tires are banned at landfills in many states because of their resiliency. Some landfills require that tires be shredded or split; others assess a fee to take them off your hands.

Needless to say, it's far better to recycle tires than to throw them into landfills to decompose for generations to come. In their next life, tires can have a number of uses, including being made into road asphalt, shoes, boat bumpers and even furniture.

The next time you purchase tires, purchase re-
treads and get the best tires you can for your
money so they will have a longer useful life. Do
properly inflate them; not only will you increase
their useful life expectancy, but you'll save gas.
It's also a good idea to rotate your tires every
6,000 miles or so, and to keep wheels properly
aligned.

CAR BATTERIES: You should not have any of
these lying around your garage. If you do, get rid
of them, but not in the landfill. Call a local automotive store or gas station to take them. That
failing, call your municipal government hazardous waste hotline or landfill for a dropsite.

MISCELLANEOUS HOUSEHOLD WASTE

YARD WASTE: Start your own backyard compost, or call your local landfill to find out if there's
a community compost you can use to dump your
greens.

DEAD ANIMALS: Call your local Animal Control
to find out how to dispose of dead animals. DO
NOT throw in your trash can.

HUMAN OR ANIMAL EXCREMENT: Try composting animal waste by burying in flower, shrub,
and tree areas. You should never compost dog
or cat excrement in your vegetable garden, however.

Animal feces can be flushed down the toilet. This

is likewise true of human feces from disposable or cloth diapers.

HYPODERMIC NEEDLES WITH SYRINGES: It's a health hazard to dispose of hypodermic needles in your regular garbage can. Since you can't recycle them either, ask your health care provider if they will accept your old needles for disposal. Or, contact your local government Health Department for a list of medical waste facilities that will take them.

APPLIANCES: A simple call to a scrap dealer or thrift reseller should take care of any refrigerators or stoves you want removed from your premises. Some scrap dealers, however, might not take appliances manufactured before 1979, when the EPA banned PCBs — or *polychlorinated biphenyls*. Appliance motors made with PCBs need to be removed from the appliance to be scrapped. CFC (*chlorofluorocarbon*) — the coolant in freezers, refrigerators, and air conditioners — will also need to be removed and disposed of properly.

CHRISTMAS TREES: Dead Christmas trees make great mulch for landscaping after they've been run through a "chipper." Many local landfills sponsor this annual activity, and have dropoff days when you can dispose of your Christmas tree for mulching. Call to find out.

If you bought a live Christmas tree but have no place in your yard to plant it (perhaps the many Christmas trees of the past have already taken up any available real estate!), your local land-scaping company or tree farm will likely help with finding a home for it.

OTHER MISCELLANY: If you have an item that's not mentioned here, be persistent in your search for a recycler. If it's automotive related, exhaust all outlets you've gone to in the past to recycle oil, batteries, or tires. Ask around. If it's metal or another alloy, try calling around at foundries, listed in the *Yellow Pages* under "Recycling" or "Scrap Metal." Don't give up.

SAFER ALTERNATIVES TO HOUSEHOLD HAZARDS

reprinted courtesy of the City of Phoenix, Arizona
Public Works-Solid Waste Management, Household Hazardous Waste Program

PRODUCT	HAZARDOUS INGREDIENTS	POSSIBLE DANGERS	USE THESE SAFER ALTERNATIVES
Aerosol sprays	butanol, butane, propanol	flammable, explosive	pump-type sprays, brush or roll-on applicators, potpourri
Ammonia-based cleaners	ammonia, ethanol	irritant, toxic, corrosive	vinegar, salt & water for surfaces. Baking soda & water for bathroom
Disinfectants	diethylene glycol, sodium hypochlorite, phenols	corrosive, toxic	1/2 cup borax in 1 gallon water
Drain openers	sodium hypochlorite, sodium/potassium hydroxide	corrosive, toxic	plunger; flush with boiling water, 1/2 cup baking soda, & 1/2 cup vinegar
Flea repellent	carbamates, organophosphate, pyrethrins	toxic	eucalyptus leaves where pet sleeps, brewer's yeast in diet
Floor & furniture polishes	diethylene glycol, petroleum distillates, nitrobenzene	flammable, toxic	1 part lemon juice with 2 parts olive or vegetable oil
Furniture strippers	acetone, methylethyl ketone, toluene, xylenes	flammable, toxic	sandpaper
Latex paints	resins, glycol, ethers, esters	flammable, toxic	lime stone-based white-wash or casein-based paint
Oil-based paints	ethylene, aliphathydrocarbons, petroleum distillates	flammable, toxic	latex or water-based paints
Oven cleaners	potassium/sodium, hydroxide, ammonia, lye	corrosive, toxic	baking soda & water, salt on spills still warm
Rat & mouse killers	lead arsenate, coumarins (warfarin), strychnine	toxic	remove food & water sources, clear nests, cover holes & drains, use mechanical traps
Roach & ant killers	organophosphates, carbamates	toxic	roaches: traps, boric acid; ants: chili pepper/cream of tarter in ants' path
Rug & upholstery cleaners	napthalene, oxalic acid, diethylene glycol	irritant, toxic, corrosive	dry corn starch or baking soda sprinkled on rug, then vacuumed
Toilet bowel cleaners	muriatic or oxalic acid, paradichlorobenzene, calcium hypochlorite	irritant, toxic, corrosive	toilet brush & baking soda; mild detergent

Part Four

Recycling At Work

Visionaries picture the workplace of the future to be paperless, which would make a lot of people (and trees!) happy. Thanks in part to the momentum of the Information Age, there are already signs of an office entirely devoid of paper.

Storing data files on computer tape, CD-ROM or diskette has become far more economical than keeping roomfuls of information on paper, and most companies today wouldn't store information any other way. In much the same way, companies are relaying information electronically. In the future, sales brochures no longer will be printed, they will be animated on-screen; production schedules no longer will be typed on paper, they will be shown in graph form on the computer. And the interoffice typewritten memo will become a thing of the past. Companies today have or are considering e-mail (electronic mail) to shuttle interoffice information from computer workstation to computer workstation.

The entirely paperless office is certainly just over the horizon. But in the meantime, the computer revolution is doing little to stop the mounting paper problem in this country. There is more paper being dumped in landfills than ever before, and the amount of paper being tossed is outpacing the growth of the waste stream. Businesses also contribute other materials to the waste stream in the form of printer cartridges, carbonless paper, *chlorofluorocarbons* (CFCs), and much more.

One defense is to recycle. Some businesses simply do not have a choice; some state and city laws require businesses to recycle paper.

If your company doesn't have a recycling program, perhaps you can bring what you've learned at home to the workplace. Your boss might even appreciate your efforts since recycling makes good environmental as well as economic sense. Recycling programs coupled with source reduction save companies millions of dollars each year.

THE SIX-STEP PLAN

You'll need to do very little planning to get a recycling program up and running at your office or place of business.

1. Start by contacting your local Public Works department. Ask if there are programs to help you. If possible, hire a recycling service. A good service will make the program run smoother and will save your company having to drop off or arrange for pickup of materials. Investigate recycling services in the *Yellow*

Pages under "Recycling Centers," or ask around.

2. Evaluate what can be recycled by performing a waste audit. Walk through the stockroom, cafeteria, production area, shipping room, and all departments. Make a list of possible recyclable items as you go. You might find these items on your list: pop cans or bottles, paper cups, newspapers, magazines, mixed paper, computer paper, packing materials, and printer cartridges (which can be refilled instead of thrown away).

3. Discuss recycling with your custodial staff or contract cleaning service. Find out what they can feasibly take on as far as collecting materials. Ask questions about how involved, if at all, they want to become. If you have a cleaning service, be sure to ask if recycling will affect the cost of your cleaning contract.

4. Set up recycling bins. For paper, you might want to put large bins near the copy machine and in the computer room, and put small baskets at each desk. According to the National Office Paper Recycling Project, a joint effort by private companies and public interest groups to maximize the recycling of office paper, companies find participation increases when collection begins at the desk.

IMPORTANT NOTE: Check local fire codes before stockpiling paper anywhere.

5. Get employees involved. Circulate a memo (on

e-mail, if you have this available to you!) asking for employee participation and input. Don't forget to promote recycling in the company newsletter, and to reward employees for their participation. As recycling matures at your company, so will employee participation.

6. Find a taker for office materials in much the same way you found a recycler for your home materials. Keep in mind your company will have more volume, and therefore could be more valuable to recyclers. Also, don't undersell computer paper. It is in high demand because of its strong fiber content.

FINDING MATERIAL VENDORS

Conduct a survey of potential vendors for your company's materials by calling around or asking other businesses in the same complex. You will find listings under "Recycling Services," "Wastepaper Dealers" or "Waste Haulers" in the *Yellow Pages.*

Questions to ask in your survey:

Are there any hauling charges? Will the dealer pay for your haul?

What grades of paper are collected and what are the specific descriptions?

Are pickups scheduled, or as needed?

Will the dealer provide recycling bins?

Will the dealer require a loading dock?

What are the hauling requirements?

Some paper recyclers take a minimum of 500 to 1,000 pounds per haul. To estimate when your company might reach that weight requirement, multiply the number of office employees by 0.5 pounds. Divide this figure into 500 or 1,000, depending on the allowable haul, to arrive at how many working days need to go by in order to fill the weight requirement.

Example: XYZ Company has 100 employees, each contributing a half-pound of computer paper per day to the recycling bin. If ABC Recycling Company requires a 1,000 pound haul, then it would take XYZ Company approximately 20 working days to meet this requirement.

RECYCLING INDUSTRY WASTE

Your company's industry will have a lot to do with what your company can recycle. For example, in a typical office, each employee discards a little over one pound of waste each day, half of which is recyclable paper.

In retail-related businesses, the waste is considerably higher at roughly four pounds of waste per employee each day due to the transportation packaging of goods. Wooden pallets, cardboard boxes, and plastic buckets are a few of the recyclable materials to be found at retail stores.

In food and beverage industries, estimates run as high as 14 pounds of mixed waste per day for every employee. In addition to pallets and plastic buckets, other recyclable items found in restaurants are glass, aluminum, plastic wrap, and steel containers.

If you work in a manufacturing plant, don't overlook obvious recyclables discarded in the manufacturing process, such as metals, glass, or plastics.

TYPES OF OFFICE PAPER

There are four types of paper generally found in the workplace, all of which can be recycled separately in order to make them more attractive to recyclers.

Computer paper, which typically comes in continuous feed and is white with green or blue bars on it. If you have a considerable amount of this paper, keep it separate to increase its marketability to recyclers.

White paper is white copier paper, letterhead, index stock, and envelopes without windows.

Mixed paper is colored copier paper, miscellany from junk mail, and construction paper.

Corrugated boxes, as in shipping boxes.

There are also office papers not yet allowed into the recycling loop, primarily those that contain glue or chemical coatings. A few to **NOT** include:
NCR or carbonless
Facsimile paper
Post-it™ notes
Mailing address labels

Paper Recycling Tips: Try to remove paper

clips and staples before recycling. Some recyclers will not accept paper from a laser printer, so check before adding this to your stockpile.

One solution for NCR and other papers not marketable to recyclers is to put them through the paper shredder and use as packing material.

OFFICE SOURCE REDUCTION

There are many ways you can reduce waste in your office. Here are just a few:

- Start contributing to the paperless office now by storing documents electronically instead of on paper.

- Take advantage of computer e-mail to route memos, and if you must print to paper, post the notice or let employees route one paper instead of printing copies for everyone.

- Make double-sided copies. Some copy machines are now equipped with this feature as are some laser printers. By using both sides of the paper, your company will be spending less on waste disposal, manpower, and paper. Cutting copier paper costs by 20% due to double copying is not unrealistic.

- Reuse file folders by reversing them.

- Don't include a cover sheet with every facsimile; make a note off to the side of the page being sent over the fax.

- Return shipping pallets and other materials to suppliers, so they can be used again. Indirectly, this will hedge against increased costs for goods.

- Return toner and printer cartridges to suppliers for refilling or rebuilding. There are even businesses that specialize in this service.

- Shred mixed paper to be reused as packing material, and save all incoming shipping peanuts for the same purpose.

- Cut discarded paper into squares and reuse as scrap paper and notepads.

Part Five

Buying
Recycled

When most of us think of recycling, we think of mounds of bottles, cans, or newspapers, ready to be hauled off to some place as far from our daily reality as, well, the landfill. And ironically, plenty of recyclables have been set aside, washed and sorted by impassioned recyclers only to arrive at the landfill because of this very mind-set.

Fortunately, people are realizing that to keep their recyclables marketable to manufacturers, they have to buy the recycled products manufacturers make. To close the recycling loop, we have to buy recycled. We simply cannot recycle any other way.

Still, buying recycled is a new way of thinking about recycling and a new way of purchasing goods. It's no wonder that there has been some confusion as to the quality, price and availability of recycled products.

THE TWO MOST COMMON MYTHS TO BUYING RECYCLED

MYTH: Buying recycled costs more.

False. Buying recycled can actually save you money. Although it's true that price-comparison shopping and buying recycled do not always go hand-in-hand, it's certainly not true that you will have to increase your grocery budget to close the recycling loop. Most of the "green" or recycled products on the shelf in grocery stores today are competitively priced, and a few are even less expensive than their ecologically unfriendly counterparts.

The same is true for products that do away with excessive packaging, which cost consumers dearly. Packaging makes up around 8% of the cost of goods, and when you cut packaging, you save.

MYTH: Recycled products are not as good as "regular" products.

Not true, although there used to be a small grain of truth to this. Recycled paper grocery bags, for example, used to be considered lightweight and not as sturdy as those made of virgin paper. That's now changed, thanks to advancing recycling technology. These bags can withstand the rigors of grocery hauling and are being used extensively today.

For the most part, packaging and products made from recycled material are just as good as if they had been made from virgin material. To prove it to yourself, the next time you're at the grocery store, try to determine packaging that has been made out of recycled material and packaging that has not. You'll probably be surprised. Over 50% of the aluminum for cans is made from recycled aluminum, for example, and most cereal boxes are made of recycled paper. The irony is that because most of us can't tell, it's hard for us to shop recycled.

CONSUMER GUIDELINES

Over 20,000 new products arrive on the supermarket shelf each year, making buying recycled as formidable a task as comparing labels and price.

But don't worry. You needn't be at the store all day weighing budget, health, and now ecological considerations for every item you want to put into your cart. In fact, after you've collected recyclables for a few weeks, you'll begin to notice the materials that you can't recycle and those you can. Soon, buying recycled will become almost second-nature to you. Until then, you can always take comfort in knowing that there are a few guidelines.

Watch for green standards

Wouldn't it be great if the government had some sort of ecology rating system for purchasing goods, and you could shop for recycled much like you shop for price? That hasn't happened yet, but there are standards in place that can give you a reading on what's what on the grocery shelf.

The most popular is the recycling logo. The logo of three chasing arrows symbolizes that the product is made from recycled materials, or can be recycled. The three arrows on a dark background signify the product is made from recycled materials and is, of course, recyclable. The three arrows with no background signify the product is recyclable.

The sign for recyclable.

The sign for recycled.

There also are certification marks you can look for in a product. Look for seals of approval by Green Cross or Green Seal, two independent American companies that test products and packaging according to environmental qualities. There are others that also offer some guidelines, including the Federal government. In July of 1992, the Federal Trade Commission established ecology advertising and labeling guidelines to help consumers make purchasing decisions. Take advantage of these guidelines, but with caution. These guidelines are voluntary and there are few restrictions in manufacturers' use of them.

Degradable, biodegradable and photodegradable

which means the product will break down in a reasonable time if given enough light, air and/or water. But careful here: not everyone agrees that landfills are good environments for decomposition of these types of products (see side bar "Fast-Degradable Vs. Non-Degradable").

Recyclable

which means the product can be recovered for use as raw material in the manufacture or assembly of a new product or package.

Compostable

which means all materials in the product will break down into usable compost given compost conditions.

Recycled Content

which means the product has been made from materials that were recovered from the waste stream, either pre- or post-consumed. Post-consumed paper is basically paper already used, and pre-consumed paper is paper scrapped by printers. Post-consumed is a better ecological buy.

Buy according to the highest level of recyclability

Some materials can be recycled almost indefinitely, and other materials have a limited recyclable lifespan.

Whenever possible, buy products with the highest level of recyclability.

Glass bottles, for example, can be used over and over again for the same purpose. That's why just about every glass jar or bottle you see on the grocery shelf is made from at least 20% recycled glass.

Glass, whatever form, is 100% recyclable. It doesn't lose any of its properties each time it is reclaimed, but stays consistent whether it's been made into a jar the first time or the 200th time.

The same can't be said for too many of the recyclable commodities, although a few come close. Aluminum cans go through a reclamation process to be made into other aluminum cans, so if you're buying beverages in aluminum cans and recycling them, you're helping to use this resource wisely. Products packaged in paper also are good choices, but try to avoid paper with coated stock. As technology stands today, these papers are harder to recycle than other, less decorated papers.

Plastics can be a good ecological choice in some cases, but plastics typically are reclaimed a limited number of times and for very few products. For sanitary reasons, reclaimed plastic soda bottles aren't yet used to make other plastic soda bottles but are more often used to make trash cans, boots, toys, lawn furniture or other non-food items.

As a general rule, the products and packaging with the highest level of recyclability are made of glass, followed by aluminum, paper and then plastic.

Buy what you can recycle

Many materials can be recycled today, but not all materials can be recycled in your community. The folks in Timbucktu might be recycling glass, but that doesn't do you much good if you're miles away in a community of citizens who neither can nor want to recycle glass. If this is the case, your best bet is to buy juices and other beverages in containers made of aluminum or other materials that your community does take for recycling.

Conversely, most of us do not want to recycle every material that's being recycled in our communities. The idea then is to buy what you recycle whenever possible.

Buy products already recycled

Choose "green" packaging, or packaging that has been made from recycled materials, over packaging that is made of virgin material.

You might be able to tell if the packaging is made of recycled material by checking on the back or bottom for the recycling logo, which is three chasing arrows against a dark background. This means the packaging has been made from some recycled material, although the manufacturer is not obliged to tell you how much.

Often, the recycling logo comes with a statement such as "made from recycled material." Or, if you're purchasing a product made from recycled paper, the manufacturer usually will state on the package whether it's made from post- or pre-consumed paper and how much.

Paperboard boxes, used for cereal, pasta mixes and other food items, are likely to be made of recycled material. This will be apparent if the box has a gray interior.

Get the right paper

Recycled paper comes in two types, post-consumed or pre-consumed. Pre-consumed is unused, usually uninked paper trimmings and leftover scraps from the process of making paper. Typically, pre-consumed trimmings and leftovers come straight from the printing plant to be recycled into usable paper, or other products.

Post-consumed is used and discarded paper like stationery, newspaper, packaging, and direct mail. Whenever you have a choice, seek products made from post-consumed paper over products made from pre-consumed paper. Also, buy paper printed with vegetable-based inks whenever possible; these inks are non-toxic.

Pass by disposable products

Lose the throw-away habit. Not only are we clogging up landfills with disposable diapers, razors, coffee filters, towels, and dishware, we're spending our hard-earned money needlessly.

You don't have to do it all at once, and it doesn't

have to be an all or nothing proposition. Get your spouse a refillable razor for Christmas. Try eating your fast-food burger with a linen napkin instead of the disposable napkin it comes with (this is a great mood lifter!). Give cloth diapers a try one day a week, or for one diaper change during the day. Sound like too much of a hassle? As a working mother who used cloth while her son was in diapers, I can assure you it's not. There are now hassle-free diaper covers with Velcro™ tabs, so there are no pins for those of us with big thumbs. And there are diaper services that pick up and deliver and require no diaper rinsing on your part. You don't have to swear off disposables completely, but you don't have to use disposables exclusively either.

Check out the packaging

You're investing a lot in packaging — approximately a third of your household trash and $1 of every $12 you spend at the grocery store — so look at products with an eye for packaging.

GET RID OF THE EXCESS. Foremost on the packaging hit list is that of excessive packaging. We've all seen these: the frozen dinner that is boxed with a sauce packet put inside a tub that is covered with a plastic wrap; the fruit cups that are individually packaged and wrapped in cardboard; rice that is packaged in plastic within a box. Packaging like this is supposed to be convenient, but my experience is that packaging of this nature *appears* to be far more convenient than it really is.

AVOID COMPOSITE PACKAGING. Some packages are made from a combination of materials that are unsuitable for recycling. These are the aseptic juice boxes made from plastic, paper and aluminum. Or the squeezable ketchup bottles made from every plastic known to modern man. These materials can't easily be stripped from one another for recycling. They're simply not suitable for recycling, or for the grocery cart.

FOREGO THE WRAP FOR PRODUCE AND NON-FOOD ITEMS. Forget the packaging all together for those household products that do not need packaging for sanitary or security reasons. For example, vegetables and fruit such as squash and cantaloupe have thick rinds and don't need packaging. You could probably forego the plastic produce bag altogether and not even miss it.

SHOP FOR BULK. The more product in the package the better. That also goes for bulk foods, products you can weigh and package yourself at the store. Flour, pasta, and many other staples of the kitchen come this way, so bring your reused produce bags to package bulk items the next time you're at the store.

BUY REFILLABLE PACKAGING: Products that come in packaging you can refill time and time again are ecologically and economically smart buys.

Use common sense

The final word on green shopping and buying recycled is to use common sense. The world of recycling is constantly changing, and all of us are thinking of new and better ways to recycle. Along with this dynamic comes the responsibility to evaluate, re-evaluate and make on-going decisions about your part in the recycling process.

PLASTIC VS. PAPER GROCERY BAGS

Plastic or paper? Every person that has stood in line at the grocery story has been asked this question. But no one, it seems, has *the* answer. Even those of us who have followed the paper versus plastic grocery bag debate for some time have been struck dumb by this question. What is the correct answer?

The answer, unfortunately, is like a moving target. It changes as technology, localities, and even public relations tactics change. As recent as a year ago, paper appeared to be in the lead, having been made stronger and better as a recycled commodity. Adding to its environmental appeal was that it was deemed a more suitable landfill commodity in the event it was tossed. Then, plastic started to gain on paper with manufacturers' claims that new plastic grocery bags now were biodegradable and some even photodegradable. The race started to heat up when grocery chains everywhere began taking in used plastic bags to be recycled. But paper didn't fold under the competitive pressure. Instead, paper manufacturers began making their recycled grocery bags better and in greater quantities. And so it goes, the never-ending paper versus plastic debate.

My answer: reuse your grocery bag of choice. Some suggest we use cloth bags to tote home our groceries, but since that's not practical for those of us who do our shopping weekly, why not reuse the grocery bags brought home on a previous outing?

CLOTH VS. DISPOSABLE DIAPERS

On one side of the cloth versus disposable diaper debate is the diaper service industry with claims that one-use disposable diapers choke landfills and introduce unsanitary human excrement — with all its infectious diseases and toxins — to the landfill and ultimately to our water supplies and farm land.

On the other side is the multi-million dollar disposable diaper industry. Disposable diapers, they argue, make up only a small percentage of the current waste in landfills and do not require the use of valuable water resources or harsh chemicals to clean them.

Neither of these arguments, however, is as persuasive as the one being presented by consumers: busy moms and dads simply want convenience.

What's a mother — or father — to do?

My answer: cloth diapers for use at home and disposables for trips away from home. While you're away at the mall or at the park, enjoy the convenience of disposables. When you're at home, change your little one into cloth. A diaper service can pick up, clean and drop off cloth diapers — and instead of safety pins, parents can now use Velcro™ covers.

This dual diaper approach adds up to good economic and environmental sense for you and your baby.

FAST-DEGRADABLE VS. NON-DEGRADABLE

It's hard to believe biodegradable and photodegradable garbage bags, diapers, and other products might be unsavory environmentally. After all, the very words biodegradable and photodegradable conjure up images of a future in which we have no worries about what we buy, consume or toss.

Yet, some of these fast-degradable plastics can be downright unfriendly to the environment, particularly if you use them carelessly or in greater numbers than you would have otherwise. Biodegradable products contain plastic mixed with cornstarch or vegetable oil. With this added ingredient, decomposition time can be dramatically reduced to as little as three years compared to 300 years without. In much the same way, photodegradable products decompose faster because of light-sensitive additives that have been added to the plastic mix. But the problem is that landfill conditions are not ideal for decomposition because oxygen, water, and light aren't likely to reach these products. What's more, some environmentalists claim that should these plastics break down in the landfill, they could prove toxic to our soil and air.

Until the science of fast-degradable products reaches maturity, my suggestion is to buy these products with great caution.

Part Six

25 Ways
You Can
Reduce Waste

Source reduction makes sense all the way around. If you don't buy what you don't need, you will not have to pay for it, sort through it, dispose of it, and ultimately all of us will not have to pay for it environmentally. Here are 25 ways you can reduce waste:

1 Remove your name from the lists of direct mail companies. Write:

Mail Preference Service
Direct Marketing Association
P.O. Box 9008
Farmingdale, NY 11735-9008

2 Recycle plastic bags by washing and drying them between use.

3 Recycle your old toothbrush by using it as an eyebrow brush, or as a bottle brush.

4 The next time you change your fish tank, douse your plants with the water. Aquarium water is good for plants.

5 Rent seldom-used power tools and appliances. Same with formal wear, glassware, silver, and china for those special occasions.

6 Fertilize your plants with used coffee grounds. Just add to the soil after cooled.

7 Glass jars are great for storing flour, nuts, nails, and other such items.

8 Reuse plastic picnic ware. After each use, rinse and store again for your next outing.

9 Instead of buying specialized containers for left-overs, reuse plastic butter and yogurt tubs for this purpose.

10 Save scraps of paper in a shoe box near the phone books to write down lists, notes, phone messages. Great use for junk mail!

11 Wrapping paper and greeting cards can be used again and again!

12 Pass on your magazines and other reading material to clinics, nursing homes, child care centers.

13 Cut up old bedding and towels to be used as cleaning rags.

14 Spread fireplace ashes on flower or vegetable beds, or save for your compost. Wood ashes are rich in potassium, food plants thrive on.

15 Give any leftover automotive cleaners such as carburetor cleaners to your local mechanic, or high-school auto class. Charity car washes will also appreciate any unused car wax you might have.

16 Ask the fast-food attendant not to double bag your order. Forks and spoons also can be eliminated in some cases. Save unused napkins or sauce packets for later.

17 Invest in rechargeable batteries and a recharger. One-time use batteries contain substances toxic to our environment and are a poor use of our resources. Plus, rechargeable batteries cost less overall.

18 Old thermometers with mercury in them might be useful to your dentist, since dentists use some mercury in tooth fillings.

19 Dry cleaners use plenty of coat hangers, so bring back your hangers every time you pick up clothes.

20 Write your grocery list on used cereal box cardboard before recycling. The cardboard will prop up easily in your shopping cart, and you can clip coupons to it.

21 Buy a permanent, reusable coffee filter, or reuse disposable coffee filters one more time before tossing.

22 Save the plastic dinner plates from frozen dinners and reuse for picnics, or to freeze your own frozen dinners.

23 Aluminum foil can be reused again and again if washed first.

24 Rinse and dry plastic wraps produce comes in from the store and collect on a paper towel spool.

25 Turn old unused clothing into quilts. One of the best presents I received was a quilt made from my husband's old baby clothes.

RESOURCES

STATE AGENCIES

Contact your state recycling agency to find out more about recycling in your local community.

ALABAMA

Department of Environmental Management
Solid Waste Branch, Land Division
17151 Congressman W.L. Dickinson Dr.
Montgomery, AL 36130
(205) 271-7700

ALASKA

Department of Environmental Conservation
Recycling Division
P.O. Box O
Juneau, AK 99811-1800
(907) 465-2600

ARIZONA

Department of Environmental Quality
Waste Planning Section
2005 North Central, Ste. 1200
Phoenix, AZ 85012
(602) 207-2300

ARKANSAS

Pollution Control & Ecology
Solid Waste Management Division
8001 National Dr.
Little Rock, AR 72219
(501) 562-7444

CALIFORNIA

Department of Conservation
Division of Recycling
819 19th Street
Sacramento, CA 95814
(916) 323-3743

COLORADO
Department of Health
Hazardous Materials & Waste Management Division
4210 East 11th Ave., Ste 351
Denver, CO 80220
(303) 331-4830

CONNECTICUT
Department of Recycling
165 Capitol Ave.
Hartford, CT 06106
(203) 566-8722

DELAWARE
Department of Natural Resources & Environmental Control
Division of Air & Waste Management
89 Kings Hwy.
Dover, DE 19903
(302) 739-3820

DISTRICT OF COLUMBIA
Office of Recycling
65 K Street, Lower Level
Washington, DC 20002
(202) 939-7116

FLORIDA
Department of Environmental Regulation
Division of Waste Management
2600 Blair Stone Rd.
Tallahassee, FL 32399
(904) 488-0300

GEORGIA
Department of Natural Resources
Environmental Protection Division
3420 Norman Berry Dr., 7th Floor
Hapeville, GA 30354
(404) 656-2836

HAWAII
Department of Health
Solid & Hazardous Waste Division
5 Waterfront Pl.
Honolulu, HI 96813
(808) 543-8227

IDAHO
Division of Environmental Quality
Hazardous Materials Branch
1410 North Hilton
Boise, ID 83706
(208) 334-5840

ILLINOIS
Office of Solid Waste & Renewable Resources
325 West Adams St., Ste. 300
Springfield, IL 62704
(217) 524-5454

INDIANA
Department of Environmental Management
Office of Solid & Hazardous Waste Management
105 South Meridian St.
Indianapolis, IN 46206
(317) 232-8883

IOWA
Department of Natural Resources
Waste Management Authority Division
900 East Grand Ave.
Des Moines, IA 50319
(515) 281-4968

KANSAS
Department of Health & Environment
Department of Solid Waste Management
Forbes Field, Bldg. 740
Topeka, KS 66620
(913) 296-1500

KENTUCKY

Division of Waste Management
Resources Recovery Branch
18 Reilly Rd.
Frankfort, KY 40601
(502) 564-6716

LOUISIANA

Department of Environmental Quality
P.O. Box 44066
Baton Rouge, LA 70804
(504) 342-9103

MAINE

Waste Management Agency
State House Station #154
Augusta, ME 04333
(207) 289-5300

MARYLAND

Department of Environmental Quality
Environmental Service
2020 Industrial Dr.
Annapolis, MD 21401
(301) 974-3291

MASSACHUSETTS

Department of Environmental Protection
Division of Solid Waste Management
1 Winter St., 3rd Floor
Boston, MA 02108
(617) 292-5980

MICHIGAN

Department of Natural Resources
Waste Management Division
P.O. Box 30028
Lansing, MI 48909
(517) 373-2730

MINNESOTA

Office of Waste Management
1350 Energy Lane, Ste. 201

St. Paul, MN 55108
(612) 649-5750

MISSISSIPPI
Department of Environmental Quality
Office of Pollution Control
P.O. Box 10385
Jackson, MS 39289
(601) 961-5171

MISSOURI
Department of Natural Resources
P.O. Box 176
Jefferson City, MO 65102
(314) 751-3176

MONTANA
Department of Health & Environmental Science
Solid & Hazardous Waste Bureau
Cogswell Bldg.
Helena, MT 59620
(406) 444-2821

NEBRASKA
Department of Environmental Control
Litter Reduction & Recycling Program
P.O. Box 98922
Lincoln, NE 68509
(402) 471-4210

NEVADA
Office of Community Services
Energy Extension Services
1100 East Williams St., Ste. 108
Carson City, NV 89710
(702) 885-4908

NEW HAMPSHIRE
Environmental Services Department
Waste Management Division
6 Hazen Dr.
Concord, NH 03301
(603) 271-2900

NEW JERSEY
Department of Energy
Office of Recycling
101 Commerce St.
Newark, NJ 07102
(201) 648-1978

NEW MEXICO
Environmental Improvement Division
Solid Waste Bureau
1190 St. Francis Dr.
Santa Fe, NM 87503
(505) 827-2959

NEW YORK
Department of Environmental Conservation
Waste Reduction & Recycling
50 Wolfe Rd., Ste. 230
Albany, NY 12233
(518) 457-7337

NORTH CAROLINA
Solid Waste Section
P.O. Box 27687
Raleigh, NC 27611
(919) 733-0692

NORTH DAKOTA
Department of Health
Division of Waste Management
P.O. Box 5520
Bismark, ND 58502
(701) 224-2366

OHIO
Litter Prevention & Recycling
Department of Natural Resources
1889 Fountain Square, Bldg. F2
Columbus, OH 43224
(614) 265-6353

OKLAHOMA
Department of Health
Solid Waste Division
1000 N.E. 10th St.
Oklahoma City, OK 73152
(405) 271-7159

OREGON
Department of Environmental Quality
Waste Reduction Division
811 S.W. 6th Ave.
Portland, OR 97204
(503) 229-5913

PENNSYLVANIA
Department of Environmental Resources
Bureau of Waste Management
P.O. Box 2063
Harrisburg, PA 17105
(717) 787-7382

RHODE ISLAND
Department of Environmental Management
83 Park St.
Providence, RI 02903
(401) 277-3434

SOUTH CAROLINA
Bureau of Solid & Hazardous Waste
2600 Bull St.
Columbia, SC 29201
(803) 734-5200

SOUTH DAKOTA
Department of Water & Natural Resources
Waste Management Program
523 East Capitol St.
Pierre, SD 57501
(605) 773-3153

TENNESSEE
Department of Health & Environment
Solid Waste Management Division
701 Broadway, Rm 160

Nashville, TN 37219
(615) 741-3424

TEXAS
Department of Health
Division of Solid Waste Management
1100 West 49th St.
Austin, TX 78756
(512) 458-7271

UTAH
Department of Environmental Quality
288 North 1460 West
Salt Lake City, UT 84116
(801) 538-6170

VERMONT
Department of Environmental Conservation
Solid Waste Division
103 South Main St.
Waterbury, VT 05676
(802) 244-7831

VIRGINIA
Department of Waste Management
101 North 14th St., 11th Floor
Richmond, VA 23219
(804) 255-2667

WASHINGTON
Department of Ecology
Recycling Information Office
4407 Woodview Dr. S.E.
Lacey, WA 98503
(206) 459-6731

WEST VIRGINIA
Division of Natural Resources
State Capital Complex, Bldg. 3 Rm. 669
1356 Hansford St.
Charleston, WV 25305
(304) 348-5929

WISCONSIN
Department of Natural Resources
Bureau of Solid & Hazardous Waste Management
P.O. Box 7921
Madison, WI 53707
(608) 267-7566

WYOMING
Department of Environmental Quality
Solid Waste Management
122 West 25th St.
Cheyenne, WY 82002
(307) 777-7752

HELPFUL ORGANIZATIONS

Here are just a few of the helpful organizations you can contact if you want to become more involved in recycling.

Citizens Clearinghouse for Hazardous Waste
2316 Wilson Blvd., Ste. A
Arlington, VA 22216
(703) 276-7070

Coalition for Recyclable Waste
5380 Repecho Dr.
San Diego, CA 92124

Environmental Defense Fund
257 Park Ave. S.
New York, NY 10010
(212) 505-2100
INFORMATION HOTLINE: (800) CALL-EDF

U.S. Environmental Protection Agency (EPA)
Office of Solid Waste Management
401 M Street S.W.
Washington, DC 20460
(202) 260-2080
INFORMATION HOTLINE: (800) 424-9346

Everything Earthly
414 South Mill Ave. #118
Tempe, AZ 85281
(800) 968-0690

Greenpeace U.S.A.
1436 U Street N.W.
Washington, DC 20009
(202) 462-1177

Inform
381 Park Ave. S., Ste. 1201
New York, NY 10016
(212) 689-4040

Keep America Beautiful
9 West Broad St.
Stamford, CT 06902
(203) 323-8987

ENVIRONMENTAL CATALOGS

Co-op America
2100 M Street N.W. Ste. 403
P.O. Box 18217
Washington, DC 20036
(202) 223-1881
FAX: (202) 728-9537

Real Goods
966 Mazzoni St
Ukiah, CA 95482-3471
(800) 762-7325
FAX: (707) 468-0301

Seventh Generation
Dept. GM
Colchester, VT 05446-1672
(802) 655-3116

MAGAZINES

BioCycle
419 State Ave
Emmaus, PA 18049
(215) 967-4135

Buzzworm: The Environmental Journal
2305 Canyon Blvd., Ste. 206
Boulder, CO 80302
(303) 442-1969

Garbage
2 Main St.
Gloucester, MA 01930
(508) 283-3200

Recycling Times
1730 Rhode Island Ave NW, Ste. 1000
Washington, DC 20036
(202) 861-0708

Recycling Today
4012 Bridge Ave
Cleveland, OH 44113
(216) 961-4130

Resource Recycling
P.O. Box 10540
Portland, OR 97210
(800) 227-1319

Waste Age
1730 Rhode Island Ave NW
Washington, DC 20036
(202) 861-0708

RECOMMENDED BOOKS

Backyard Composting: Your Complete Guide to Recycling Yard Clippings. Harmonious Technologies.

Complete Trash: The Best Way to Get Rid of Practically Everything Around the House. By M.Evans & Company, Inc.

The Green Consumer. By John Elkington, Julia Hailes and Joel Makower. Penguin Books.

The Green Pages. Your Everyday Shopping Guide to Environmentally Save Products. By the Bennett Information Group. Random House.

Rubbish! The Archaeology of Garbage. By William Rathjie and Cullen Murphy. HarperPerennial.

Save Money and Save the Earth. By Kathi A. Haas. Marketing Methods Press.

The Recycler's Handbook. By The Earth Works Group. EarthWorks Press.

Environmental Almanac. By World Resources Institute. Houghton Mifflin Company.

INDEX